I0413274

TABLE OF CONTENTS

INTRODUCTION

In the decades following World War II, a dramatic reorganization of the political landscape in Southeast Asia occurred. Four years of oppression by the Japanese triggered increased feelings of nationalism and created independence movements in many of the European and American colonies. When France, Great Britain, the Netherlands, and the United States, failed to stem the rising tides of independence in Southeast Asia, former colonies became new nation states. In addition to the former colonies achieving independence, Mao Zedong and his communist forces defeated Chiang Kai-Shek and his nationalist forces to establish the People's Republic of China. Chiang Kai-Shek and the Nationalist Party retreated to the island of Formosa and established his government there. The former colonies, the People's Republic of China, and the Republic of China began to claim areas in the resource rich South China Sea to increase their overall economic and political stature. The leadership of these nations used historical records to maximize the extent of their claims. These national claims extended past the previously established customary three nautical mile limit and placed these nations in direct competition with one another. The competing claims of these nations form the basis of the current sovereignty disputes within the South China Sea.

Chiang Kai-Shek and the Republic of China staked the first claim to the resource rich South China Sea after World War II. In 1947, Chiang Kai-Shek's government issued a map demarking Nationalist China's claim over areas inside the South China Sea. Chiang Kai-Shek's government drew an 11-dot line that encompassed the entirety of the South China Sea, claiming this area as territory of the Republic of China. Following the Communist defeat of the Nationalists in 1949, Chou Enlai, the first premier of the People's Republic of China, amended the Nationalist Chinese claim by deleting the portion of the 11-dot line extending into the Gulf of Tonkin and used the new map to establish the People's Republic of China's current claim. The

1

Republic of China also adopted this new 9-dot line, which now serves as both the People's Republic of China and Taiwan's claim.[1] Many of the Western powers ignored both Nationalist and Communist Chinese claims. The Western powers focused their attention on maintaining their colonial empires in Southeast Asia. If the Western powers had identified the potential for conflict incident to the Communist and Nationalist claims, then the Western powers might have adjudicated the issue of sovereignty in the South China Sea in the 1952 San Francisco Peace Treaty. The treaty, however, only addressed the sovereign territory of Japan.

The Allies and Japan did not sign the formal peace treaty ending the war in the Pacific until April 28, 1952. The Peace Treaty with Japan, known as the San Francisco Treaty, forced Japan to renounce all claims in the South China Sea including "all right, title and claim to the Spratly Islands and to the Paracel Islands."[2] These two island chains comprise the majority of land inside the South China Sea. The San Francisco Treaty failed to address who owned the islands. By failing to delineate ownership in 1952, the newly independent nations of the Philippines (1946), Indonesia (1949), Vietnam (1954), and Malaysia (1957) staked their own claims to these islands. With these claims, each nation sought to improve their overall national strength, especially in relation to the People's Republic of China. Claiming large portions of the South China Sea increased individual national power. These same nations also created the Association of Southeast Asian Nations (ASEAN) to increase their collective power.

On August 8, 1967, Indonesia, Malaysia, Philippines, Singapore, and Thailand established the Association of Southeast Asian Nations (ASEAN) to address regional concerns, foster economic growth, promote regional stability, and enable active collaboration among its members. Since ASEAN's inception in 1967, Brunei, Vietnam, Laos, Myanmar, and Cambodia

---

[1] Peter J. Brown, "Calculated Ambiguity in the South China Sea," *The Asia Times Online* December 8, 2009. http://www. http://www.atimes.com/atimes/Southeast_Asia/KL08Ae01.html (accessed December 13, 2012).

[2] "Treaty of Peace with Japan (with two declarations)," September 8, 1951. Chapter 2, Article 2(f).

have joined. The ASEAN states, the People's Republic of China, and Taiwan encircle the South China Sea. With five of the ten ASEAN members involved in the South China Sea dispute, a peaceful resolution would accomplish many of ASEAN's founding objectives. However, the South China Sea dispute continues and ASEAN has not offered a solution. In the absence of a collective diplomatic solution, the competing nations have used military forces from time-to-time to assert or defend their claims.[3]

In 1974, Chinese and Vietnamese sailors battled over a portion of the Paracel Islands. The battle, a Chinese victory, resulted in 146 casualties, and over 160 personnel missing. China and Vietnam fought again in 1988, over a portion of the Spratly Islands. In that battle, China swiftly defeated Vietnam, killing 74 Vietnamese sailors[4]. In addition to armed hostilities, there have been incidents during which military vessels attacked and harassed civilian or scientific vessels. In the majority of these incidents, Chinese forces were the primary aggressor. Chinese vessels have harassed scientific research vessels, detained Filipino fishermen, and intimidated research vessels from a joint Vietnamese and Indian petroleum company[5]. The sometimes violent nature of the South China Sea dispute continues to impede achievement of ASEAN's stated goals. It could also restrict transit on world's most important trade routes.

The primary shipping route from the Indian Ocean to the Pacific Ocean passes through the South China Sea. Armed conflict and harassment of civilian vessels could disrupt this major sea line of communication. This fact increased the number of actors interested in a solution. The increased involvement by nations outside the region transformed this dispute from a regional into

---

[3] "Association of Southeast Asian Nations: History," http://www.asean.org/asean/about-asean/history (accessed October 10, 2012).

[4] Jeff W. Brown, Lt Cdr, USN, "South China Sea: A History of Armed Conflict," *U.S. Naval Institute Online* (June 20, 2012, http://news.usni.org/news-analysis/news/south-china-sea-history-armed-conflict) (accessed January 21, 2013).

[5] Nitin Gokhale, "India, China Show Military Grit" *The Diplomat Online,* December 22, 2011. http://thediplomat.com/2011/12/22/india-china-show-military-grit/ (accessed January 18, 2013).

global issue. As a regional body governing five of the seven nations in dispute over the South China Sea, ASEAN faces increased pressure to construct a solution. As the United States shifts priority towards the Asia-Pacific region,[6] the United States will urge ASEAN to provide a solution to the South China Sea conflict in the best interest of the United States, its allies, and its partners in the region. Simultaneously, China will not want ASEAN involved in finding a solution. The emergence of the United States as an actor in the South China Sea dispute places ASEAN between the policies of the United States and China. The increased involvement by the world's sole superpower, the United States, and the continued involvement of the dominant regional actor, the People's Republic of China, makes clear that the South China Sea dispute is now a global problem. The escalation of this dispute from regional to global level raises the question, why have the members of ASEAN not adopted a common policy towards territorial claims in the South China Sea?

Determining why ASEAN had not adopted a common policy on the South China Sea involved answering several related questions. First, it was important to understand the strategic importance of the South China Sea, not only to the members of ASEAN but also to the world as a whole. Next, it was necessary to determine how the nations involved had pursued their claims. Finding that answer required the examination of diplomatic actions the individual claimants took. Those actions were ostensibly guided by the two international documents that set procedures for adjudicating the South China Sea dispute: the 1982 United Nations Convention on the Law of the Sea (UNCLOS) and the 2002 ASEAN Declaration on the Conduct of Parties in the South China Sea. Although each document provided a method by which to formulate solutions to the South China Sea dispute, ASEAN has still been unable to construct a solution. Since legal and political guidelines have not provided a solution, the next step was to analyze the nations, their claims, the

---

[6] U.S. Department of Defense, *Sustaining U.S. Global Leadership: Priorities for 21st Century Defense* (Washington, DC: Government Printing Office, 2012), 2.

basis of their claims, and to infer therefrom why ASEAN has not produced a collective position on the claims.

Separating the parties of the South China Sea dispute into two different groups based on their claims facilitated an analysis of each nation's claims, the justification for the claim, and the perceived benefit of the claim. The first group, referred to as the primary actors, included China, Taiwan, Malaysia, Philippines, Vietnam, Brunei, and Indonesia. Each actor in this group claimed portions of the South China Sea or of the Spratly and Paracel Islands. The second group, referred to as the secondary actors, included the remaining members of ASEAN (Cambodia, Laos, Myanmar, and Thailand) along with the United States of America and India. The second group places no physical claims to the South China Sea or the island groups but is influential in the adjudication process. Dissecting the claims and justifications offered by each nation produced an explanation of why the 1982 UNCLOS and 2002 ASEAN Declaration did not provide a solution.

The failure of the 1982 UNCLOS and the 2002 ASEAN Declaration to provide a solution does not explain why ASEAN has not developed a common position to reconcile the competing claims of its members. To explain why the members of ASEAN cannot adopt a common solution for the South China Sea dispute it was necessary to analyze the interaction of the ASEAN nations themselves. Mancur Olson's book *The Logic of Collective Action* and Alan Lamborn's article, "Theory and the Politics in World Politics," offered insight into the dynamics of group decision making and international relations. Using these two theories to analyze the South China Sea dispute led to the realization that ASEAN cannot adopt a common solution because the nations involved in the dispute value their own self-interests over a collective solution.

THE STRATEGIC IMPORTANCE OF THE SOUTH CHINA SEA

Seven nations have claims within the South China Sea. To determine the purpose and legitimacy of each country's claim required answering three questions. First, how does the overall geography of the region shape its strategic value? Next, what is the economic value of the resources in and under the South China Sea as well as the trade that transits it? Last, was how does the geography and economic value the South China Sea increase or decrease its military value? The answers to these questions explained why each nation placed its claim and justified creating a solution that solely benefited its people.

The United Nations Convention on the Law of the Sea (UNCLOS) defined the South China Sea as a semi-enclosed sea. Article 122 of the 1982 UNCLOS defined a semi-enclosed sea as "a gulf, basin or sea surrounded by two or more States and connected to another sea or the ocean by a narrow outlet."[7] China, the Philippines, Brunei, Malaysia, Indonesia, and Vietnam surround the South China Sea and the Straits of Taiwan and Malacca provide access to the South China Sea from the northwest and southeast respectively. Inside the South China Sea lie two large island groups, the Spratly and Paracel Islands, of which China, Vietnam, Malaysia, and the Philippines each claim portions. The Spratly Islands are located in the southern portion of the South China Sea near Brunei, Indonesia and the Philippines and border one of the primary shipping routes through the South China Sea. Ships entering the South China Sea via the Strait of Malacca en route to Japan use the shipping lane that borders the Spratly Islands. In the northern portion of the South China Sea near Vietnam and China lie the Paracel Islands. These islands border the shipping lane used when transiting the South China Sea to and from Hong Kong.[8] The topography of the South China Sea restricts large vessels to these two main shipping routes.

Vessels transiting these two shipping lanes, account for half of the world's tonnage and over ninety percent of the goods moving by ship each year. [9] Japan, South Korea, and Taiwan, three of the United States closest partners in the region, receive over 80% of the oil they import by these routes. Additionally, these ships also transport two-thirds of the world's supply of

---

[7] "United Nations Convention on the Law of the Sea," 1982. Part IX, Article 122, page 63.

[8] U.S. Pacific Command, *South China Sea Reference Book*, (Honolulu, HI, 1996), 17.

[9] Patrick M. Cronin, *Cooperation from Strength: The United States, China, and the South China Sea* (Washington, DC: Center for New American Security, 2012), 7.

Liquefied Natural Gas. In addition to the resources travelling above the water, various studies completed by different nations assess that the South China Sea holds between twenty-eight and two-hundred-thirteen billion barrels of oil (bbl.) underground. As a comparison, the United States holds roughly twenty-five bbl. (12th in the World) while Venezuela possesses 211 bbl. (2nd in the World).[10]

Coupled with the economic value of the resources that pass through the South China Sea or lie below it, the South China Sea is the fourth largest fishery in the world. This fishery provides 10% of the world and almost one-quarter of the Asian fish requirements. The value of this catch on the world market is approximately three billion dollars. Control over both the petroleum prospects and fisheries in the South China Sea would provide a substantial economic boost to the controlling party. [11] The sheer volume of these resources moving canalized on one of the two routes through the South China Sea increase the military value of the region.

The fact that the South China Sea links the Middle East and the Pacific Ocean enhances the South China Sea economic value and serves as the basis of its military value. The vessels moving on the routes through the South China Sea transport not only ninety-percent of the world goods but also transport forces for deployment of forces to the Middle East or in support of events in Southeast Asia. A force stationed at the Spratly or Paracel Islands possesses the ability to control and interdict all trade and troop deployments passing through the region, which is why the Japanese stationed a naval force here during World War II. Controlling these islands would significantly increase the political stature of such a nation or coalition. The desire to increase

---

[10] Dong Manh Nguyen "Settlement of Disputes under the 1982 United Nations Convention On the Law of the Sea: The Case of the South China Sea Dispute," (December 2005): 11.

[11] Ibid., 13.

stature led to four separate nations claim sovereignty over the Spratly Islands and Paracel Islands.[12]

The topography, economic value, and military value are why members of ASEAN and China are in dispute over control of the area. Each nation understands the tremendous strategic benefit to controlling portions of the South China Sea. The sovereignty of the Spratly and Paracel Islands in the South China Sea is a significant hurdle to overcome when creating a solution. Controlling the areas allowed by the 1982 United Nations Convention on the Law of the Sea increases the both the economy and security of each nation. However, controlling the entirety of the South China Sea would establish a nation as a regional hegemon and a potential superpower. After answering what is the strategic value of the South China Sea, the next step was to understand how the 1982 United Nations Convention on the Law of the Sea and the 2002 ASEAN Declaration on the Conduct of Parties in the South China Sea should have provided a solution.

PAPERWORK

Two documents govern the actions of the participants in the South China Sea dispute, the 1982 United Nations Convention on the Law of the Sea (UNCLOS) and the 2002 ASEAN Declaration on the Conduct of Parties in the South China Sea. The 1982 UNCLOS replaced the original 1958 UNCLOS and has broader applicability than the South China Sea. Nine of the ten members of ASEAN (Cambodia has not ratified it) and China have ratified the 1982 UNCLOS. Therefore, in this dispute the primary actors have ratified the governing treaty that provides ways to adjudicate the competing claims. Under this treaty, the members of ASEAN and China have not successfully adjudicated their claims. To control the actions of all parties until reaching a permanent solution, all members of ASEAN plus China signed the ASEAN Declaration on the

---

[12] Nguyen "Settlement of Disputes under the 1982 United Nations Convention On the Law of the Sea", 10.

8

Conduct of Parties in the South China Sea in 2002. This document is not a treaty but a political declaration and creates no legal obligation. The 2002 ASEAN Declaration provided an interim common policy that all members of ASEAN and China could operate under until reaching a permanent solution. These two documents provide the parameters for what a nation may legally claim, the processes available for resolving disputes, and an interim code of conduct until the nations reached a permanent solution.

<u>1982 United Nations Convention on the Law of the Sea</u>

The 1982 United Nations Convention on the Law of the Sea regulates maritime claims. A requirement to regulate maritime claims originated in 1945 when American President Harry Truman claimed exclusive economic rights to all natural resources on the continental shelf of the United States. Following that U.S. declaration, many other nations extended their claims leading to a worldwide dismissal of the original three nautical mile boundary agreed upon for the extension of state sovereignty. The next countries to extend their claims were all South American. Prior to 1950, Argentina, Chile, Peru, and Ecuador all extended their boundaries either to the continental shelf or to a distance of two-hundred nautical miles. In addition to extending economic boundaries, many other countries extended their territorial seas from three nautical miles from shore to twelve nautical miles. Many archipelagic nations claimed the waters separating their islands as part of the territorial seas regardless of distance. As technology advanced, nations expanded their territorial and economic claims. In 1967, Malta's ambassador to the UN called for an update to the established Law of the Sea in light of the increase in technology, the growing competition for undersea resources, and the potential for military conflict.[13]

---

[13] "The United Nations Convention On the Law of the Sea," A Historical Perspective, http://www.un.org/Depts/los/convention_agreements/convention_historical_perspective.htme (accessed September 18, 2012).

In 1973, in response to the Ambassador's plea, the Third United Nations Conference on the Law of the Sea convened in New York to address the growing threat presented by improved technology and increased pollution. From 1973 until 1982, this conference worked to create a new treaty to address the issues. In 1982, they published the United Nations Convention on the Law of the Sea.[14] The 1982 version of the UNCLOS still serves as the authoritative document on Laws of the Sea. All of the primary actors in the South China Sea dispute have ratified this treaty. Only Cambodia and the United States have failed to ratify the entirety of the 1982 UNCLOS from the secondary actor group.[15] The ratification of this treaty means the nations will abide by the regulations inside the 1982 UNCLOS.

The 1982 UNCLOS codified many of the claims made by nations following World War II and President Truman's expansion of the exclusive economic zone. The treaty provided clear legal guidance for what a nation may claim depending on distance from its coastline. With the significant increase in the area a nation may claim, the potential for overlapping claims also increased. The 1982 UNCLOS contained provisions for dispute settlement for when the claims of nations overlapped. Because the 1982 UNCLOS is the primary source governing maritime claims, most of the nations involved in the South China Sea dispute cite the treaty to justify their claims.

As outlined by the 1982 UNCLOS, a nation may claim four different zones. Each zone contains different rules and regulations concerning the status of the sea itself, the resources underneath, and transit of international vessels. The four claims a nation may make, in order of distance from the coastline, are territorial sea, contiguous zone, exclusive economic zone, and the

---

[14] "The United Nations Convention On the Law of the Sea," The Third Conference, http://www.un.org/Depts/los/convention_agreements/convention_historical_perspective.htme (accessed September 18, 2012).

[15] "Chronological Lists of Ratifications Of, Accessions and Successions to the Convention and the Related Agreements." http://www.un.org/Depts/los/reference_files/chronological_lists_of_ratifications.htm (accessed November 5, 2012).

continental shelf. A different part of the 1982 UNCLOS governs each zone and explains in detail its concept and purpose. These zones exist to improve the security and economy of the owning nation.

To increase the security of a state, a nation may claim the first twelve nautical miles from its coastline as territorial sea. A nation may enforce its national laws inside the territorial sea and the 1982 UNCLOS grants them "sovereignty to the air space over the territorial sea as well as to its bed and subsoil." Inside the territorial sea any resources in or under the sea belong solely to that nation. In addition any vessel transiting these waters or aircraft flying over them are subject to the owning nations laws. One restriction placed on the territorial sea by Part II, Section 3 of the 1982 UNCLOS is that while a nation possesses sovereignty of its territorial sea, "ships of all States, whether coastal or land-locked, enjoy the right of innocent passage through the territorial sea." The 1982 UNCLOS continues to define innocent passage in Article 19 of Section 3 as "innocent so long as it is not prejudicial to the peace, good order or security of the coastal state." For example, submarines travelling through a territorial sea must "navigate on the surface and to show their flag." [16] The territorial zone effectively increases the borders of a nation twelve miles into the sea, extending from the subsoil to the air space of above, enabling the identification of threats prior to reaching the mainland. Past the territorial sea, the next claim a nation may make is that of the contiguous zone.

The contiguous zone extends from the territorial sea to a distance of twenty-four nautical miles from a nation's coastline to increase further the security of a nation. The contiguous zone extends the ability of the nation to enforce specific laws out to a distance of twenty-four nautical miles. The contiguous zone primarily enables a nation to prosecute "infringement of the above [territorial sea] laws and regulations committed within its territory or territorial sea." The

---

[16] "United Nations Convention on the Law of the Sea," 1982. Part II, Section 1, Article 2, Point 2 page 27; Part III, Section 3, Article 19-20, page 31.

contiguous zone provides additional security to a nation by allowing them more latitude to prosecute criminals but is not as restrictive to other actors as the territorial sea. In the contiguous zone, ships that did not enter the territorial sea of another nation and only transiting this contiguous zone are not subject to the laws of the owning nation. Nations may only enforce laws in the contiguous zone that were broken inside the nation or in the territorial sea. In contrast to the territorial sea, submarines may transit the area submerged. [17] Past the areas for security, the territorial sea and contiguous zone are two areas designed to increase the economic abilities of the state

The economic exclusion zone (EEZ) is the next area a nation may claim. As defined by Part V of the 1982 UNCLOS, the EEZ borders the territorial sea (the first twelve nautical miles of the EEZ are the contiguous zone) and extends to two-hundred nautical miles from the coast. "In the exclusive economic zone, the costal state has sovereign rights for the purpose of exploring and exploiting, conserving and managing natural resources, whether living or non-living." This zone is solely for the economic benefit of the state. It exercises authority only on matters of resource-related activities, scientific research, and environmental protection. As with the contiguous zone, this area is open to freedom of navigation for all naval vessels and aircraft.[18] The final zone past the EEZ a state may claim is the continental shelf.

President Truman first claimed the continental shelf principle as an exclusive economic zone for the United States in 1945. Part VI of the 1982 UNCLOS codifies when and what a nation may claim under the continental shelf principle. The continental shelf principle can extend the EEZ to a distance of three-hundred-fifty nautical miles. A nation claiming a continental shelf must meet specific geological criteria as outlined. A nation may not simply extend their EEZ to three-hundred-fifty nautical miles; the determination for this distance resides on the content of the

---

[17] "United Nations Convention on the Law of the Sea," 1982. Part III, Section 4.

[18] "United Nations Convention on the Law of the Sea," 1982. Part V.

seabed and subsoil. Within the continental shelf zone, "the coastal Sate exercises over the continental shelf sovereign rights for the purpose of exploring it and exploring natural resources." Naval vessels and aircraft have the same rights to access as the EEZ. Since the zone a nation can claim may extend to a position 350 nautical miles from shore, the potential for overlapping claims in a semi-enclosed sea such as the South China Sea is great. The 1982 UNCLOS contains methods for adjudication of overlapping legal claims.[19]

Part XV of the UNCLOS outlines two methods for dispute settlement. First, nations may voluntarily adjudicate their competing claims and reach an agreement without involvement of the United Nations. Typically, countries resolve these disputes either through joint exploration of the area or by splitting the disputed zone in half. If the nations cannot voluntarily reach a solution, a compulsory method exists, explained by Part XV, Section 2 of the 1982 UNCLOS. Here a nation indicates through written preference which of four compulsory ways the nation prefers to use to adjudicate the dispute. A nation may elect to adjudicate a competing claim through the International Tribunal for the Law of the Sea, the International Court of Justice, an arbitral tribunal, or a special arbitral tribunal. Since a "decision rendered by a court or tribunal having jurisdiction under this section shall be final and shall be complied with by all parties to the dispute," nations very rarely use this method. Most nations prefer to use the voluntary process in order to achieve the most beneficial solution.[20]

The 1982 UNCLOS provides a legal framework under which all signatories must operate concerning maritime activities. It also codifies what a nation may claim in each zone as well as how far each zone extends. The 1982 UNCLOS even provides methods for dispute resolution when legal claims overlap. Since all the primary actors ratified the 1982 UNCLOS, ASEAN

---

[19] "United Nations Convention on the Law of the Sea," 1982. Part VI.

[20] Dong Manh Nguyen "Settlement of Disputes under the 1982 United Nations Convention On the Law of the Sea: The Case of the South China Sea Dispute," (December 2005): 32.

could use this document to create a formal solution to the South China Sea dispute. This solution would incorporate the legal authorities granted by the 1982 UNCLOS and previously agreed to by all signatories. The 1982 UNCLOS contains the requisite authorities to create a binding solution for all portions of the dispute except ownership of the Spratly and Paracel Islands. If ASEAN's members truly wanted a collective solution, they would have adjudicated their disputes using this formal process. However, they have not. This inability of ASEAN to use a legally binding document to establish a solution indicates the individual nations desires against a mutually beneficial solution. To maintain the façade of attempting to create a solution the members of ASEAN and China signed the ASEAN Declaration on the Conduct of Parties in the South China Sea in 2002. The 2002 ASEAN Declaration attempted to limit the claims the members of ASEAN and China could make in the South China Sea and the disputed territories of the Spratly and Paracel Islands. This document has less legal authority that the binding 1982 UNCLOS. The 2002 ASEAN Declaration continues the narrative of attempting a solution.

2002 ASEAN Declaration on the Conduct of Parties in the South China Sea

At the Eighth ASEAN Summit in 2002, ASEAN and China signed the ASEAN Declaration on the Conduct of Parties in the South China Sea.[21] The 2002 Declaration promotes "a peaceful, friendly and harmonious environment in the South China Sea between ASEAN and China for the enhancement of peace, stability, economic growth and prosperity in the region."[22] This declaration reiterated the words of the ASEAN charter and directly applied them towards the South China Sea dispute. As in interim solution, the 2002 Declaration had many faults and few benefits. The declaration does not possess the same legal authority as the 1982 United Nations

---

[21] "Association of Southeast Asian Nations: ASEAN Summits," http://www.asean.org/asean/asean-summit (accessed October 10, 2012).

[22] "Declaration On the Conduct of Parties in the South China Sea," http://www.asean.org/asean/external-relations/china/item/declaration-on-the-conduct-of-parties-in-the-south-china-sea (accessed December 13, 2012).

Convention on the Law of the Sea. In addition, the declaration does not present any methods to adjudicate disputes as the 1982 UNCLOS did. The 2002 Declaration attempted to clarify the further disposition of the landmasses inside the South China Sea. Since the declaration contained no provisions for resolving disputes and did not legally bind members to a solution. The 2002 Declaration failed to significantly alter the behavior of the involved nations. While ASEAN failed to leverage the 1982 UNCLOS to create a permanent solution, their attempt at an interim solution, the 2002 Declaration, also failed.

The 2002 Declaration consisted of ten separate points. The first three points in the 2002 Declaration reiterated the signatories' agreement to uphold the principles outlined in 1982 UNCLOS and other treaties governing international relations. The fourth point directly addressed how the members would resolve their dispute in accordance with the 1982 UNCLOS. In this section, the members of ASEAN and China stated their preference for the voluntary over compulsory method of dispute resolution. The agreement of the parties to the voluntary method of resolution indicated that they will not adjudicate their claims in the international courts or tribunals for binding mediation but will resolve them through other agreements. After reaffirming the adherence of the members of ASEAN and China to the legal precedents established by the 1982 UNCLOS, the next section of the 2002 Declaration addressed the conduct of parties until permanent adjudication of the competing claims.[23]

The next section attempted to correct an issues not covered by the 1982 UNCLOS or the 1952 San Francisco Treaty. Point five of the declaration stated that nations "exercise self-restraint in the conduct of activities that would complicate or escalate disputes and affect peace and stability" and refrain "from action of inhabiting on the presently uninhabited islands, reefs,

---

[23] "Declaration On the Conduct of Parties in the South China Sea," http://www.asean.org/asean/external-relations/china/item/declaration-on-the-conduct-of-parties-in-the-south-china-sea (accessed December 13, 2012).

shoals, cays, and other features and to handle their differences in a constructive manner."[24] The latter portion of this point addressed a shortcoming of the 1982 UNCLOS and an oversight by the 1952 San Francisco Treaty. The shortcoming of the 1982 UNCLOS was that it applies only to the navigable waters and does not possess any jurisdiction over the ownership of island groups or landmasses. The oversight of the 1952 San Francisco Treaty was that it only forced Japan to renounce ownership of the Spratly and Paracel Islands but did not state who would receive ownership. Preventing the habitation of islands in the Spratly and Paracel Islands effectively limited a nation's ability to claim sovereignty over the islands. The sovereignty of these islands is one of the most contested issues in the South China Sea dispute. Habitation of these islands would significantly increase the complexity of the dispute as well as increase the difficulty in designing a solution. Their sovereignty and habitability are important under Article 121 of the 1982 UNCLOS. This article did not grant sovereignty but enabled a nation to extend their EEZ from an inhabited island.[25] This extension would lead to further overlapping claims and more complexity inside the dispute.

Following point five, point six in the declaration stated how the nations would operate until resolution of the disputes. This point addressed that all signatories possess a shared responsibility to conduct many of the activities outlined by the 1982 UNCLOS. Since all of the primary actors ratified the treaty, there remains a responsibility to conduct these activities required under ownership. Most significant is the requirements to limit pollution. Concluding the declaration were four points discussing how the nations will respect the principles of the declaration.[26]

---

[24] "Declaration On the Conduct of Parties in the South China Sea," http://www.asean.org/asean/external-relations/china/item/declaration-on-the-conduct-of-parties-in-the-south-china-sea (accessed December 13, 2012).

[25] "United Nations Convention on the Law of the Sea," 1982. Article 121.

[26] "Declaration On the Conduct of Parties in the South China Sea," http://www.asean.org/asean/external-relations/china/item/declaration-on-the-conduct-of-parties-in-the-

The main value to the 2002 ASEAN Declaration generated from point five and its provision concerning the Spratly and Paracel Islands. As the members of ASEAN and China seek to extend their claims in the South China Sea, habitation of these islands will become an increasing point of contention. The 2002 Declaration also represented the first formal agreement by the members of ASEAN and China over conduct during the South China Sea dispute. The 2002 Declaration demonstrated the desire of each nation to reach a solution but provided no new method for reaching one. The current activity in the South China Sea shows that while this document provided a rationale way to move forward, none of the signatories actually abides by it.

The 1982 UNCLOS treaty provided the framework and legality for claims made by nations in the South China Sea. It outlined and explained the four zones a nation may legally claim and the authorities they may execute in each. Lastly it provided methods by which nation may adjudicate competing claims. The 2002 ASEAN Declaration provided a guideline for nations operating in the South China Sea in lieu of a permanent resolution of the dispute. It categorized how the primary actors in the dispute will conduct themselves in the South China Sea until a permanent resolution of the various disputes. It also stated that the members of ASEAN and China would resolve their disputes under the voluntary principles outlined in the 1982 UNCLOS. The fact that the 1982 UNCLOS, which possessed the weight of international law, and the 2002 Declaration could not change the behaviors of the parties involved demonstrates the complexity of this dispute. The primary actors operate to increase or maintain their original claim. No side will voluntarily decrease their claim to resolve this dispute. Since a legally binding treaty and a voluntary political agreement cannot solve the South China Sea dispute indicates that each nation perceives the perceived benefit from each claim as superior to the military clashes and civilian harassment. Each nation will continue this dispute as long as they believe a chance remains to receive the greatest result.

south-china-sea (accessed December 13, 2012).

ACTORS AND CLAIMS

Categorizing the involved nations as primary or secondary actors assisted in determining the underlying reasons for why ASEAN could not use the 1982 UNCLOS or 2002 ASEAN Declaration to reach a solution to the South China Sea dispute. The primary actors have a geographic claim in the South China Sea partially supported by the 1982 UNCLOS. This group includes China, Taiwan, Philippines, Vietnam, Malaysia, Indonesia, and Brunei. Of this group, four nations extend claims to the Spratly or Paracel Islands: China, Philippines, Vietnam, and Malaysia. The extensive area that the 1982 UNCLOS allows nations to claim and the geography of the South China Sea create a situation where the claims of the primary actors overlap. In addition to the area a nation may legally claim in accordance with the 1982 UNCLOS, China and Vietnam cite historical claims to the region and extended their claims past the exclusive economic zone and continental shelf. The 1982 UNCLOS does recognize any claim based on historical records. The number of overlapping claims and the precedent of using military forces to defend a national claim worry nations outside the region. An escalation of the current dispute would significantly affect global movement of goods and personnel. The secondary actors became involved to minimize the potential for this dispute to destabilize the region as well as the world. The United States of America, India, Cambodia, Laos, Myanmar, Singapore, and Thailand comprise the secondary actor group. These nations place no geographic claim to portions of the South China Sea and each nation maintains interest in the resolution of the South China Sea dispute for different reasons. The claims of each nation and the interaction between the nations helped explain the lack of a solution.

Primary Actors (Bordering the SCS)

The combination of the national power of the People's Republic of China and the extent of their claim in the South China Sea make it the most the most significant actor in the primary group.[27] China claims the entirety of the South China Sea to include the Spratly and Paracel Islands This claim exceeds the legal authority granted a coastal state under the 1982 UNCLOS. However, China believes the historical record of ownership supersedes the limitations placed by the 1982 UNCLOS, a treaty it ratified. China bases its claim on historical records dating to the Han Dynasty (200BC) that reference use of the area by China along with literature of that other inhabitants' acknowledged ownership of the South China Sea by China.[28] The claim to the entirety of the South China Sea as the territorial sea of China places China in a much different dispute with the remaining primary actors. The claim of the South China Sea as territorial sea versus exclusive economic zone justifies the ability of China to use force in the South China Sea to enforce its national laws. While China ignores the legal limits the 1982 UNCLOS set for a territorial sea, China uses the 1982 UNCLOS definition and regulations for a territorial sea to justify its actions inside the South China Sea. The 1982 UNCLOS allows for the use of force to patrol and evict other nation's vessels if they are in violation of Chinese law.[29] Because of China's aggressive position, it initiates the preponderance of armed incidents in the South China. The most significant of these conflicts occur with Vietnam. Vietnam asserts an identical geographic claim as China placing these two nations as the principle actors in the South China Sea dispute.

As with China, Vietnam claims the entirety of the South China Sea including the Spratly and Paracel Islands on a historical basis. To strengthen their expansive claim, both China and Vietnam have attempted to colonize portions of the Spratly and Paracel Islands. A colony on

---

[27] While two separate entities, China and Taiwan cite the same historical precedent and have the same territorial claims in the South China Sea. This study will sole focus on the actions the actions of China. The reason for focusing on China over Taiwan is that the other actors in the South China Sea dispute primarily interact with China concerning a solution.

[28] Jianming Shen, "China's Sovereignty Over the South China Sea Islands: A Historical Perspective," *Chinese Journal of International Law* (2002): 95-137.

[29] "South China Sea," http://www.eia.gov/countries/regions-topics.cfm?fips=SCS (accessed December 13, 2012).

these islands would permit the extension of a maritime claim under the 1982 UNCLOS. The 2002 ASEAN Declaration attempted to prevent this. Similar to China, Vietnam cites historical reports dating to the 17th century allowing for a claim more extensive than allowed under the 1982 UNCLOS. The primary difference in the claims between China and Vietnam is the status of the area claimed. China claims the area as a territorial sea while Vietnam claims the area as an exclusive economic zone (EEZ). Vietnam desires the area for economic reasons and does not publically express a desire to enforce its laws throughout the South China Sea.[30] Until China and Vietnam reach an agreement of their competing claims, there is no incentive for the other nations to reach an agreement between themselves because either China or Vietnam will claim the solution is not valid. One such nation is the Philippines whose claim overlaps with China, Vietnam, Indonesia, and Brunei.

The Philippines does not claim the entirety of the South China Sea as China and Vietnam do. However, like China and Vietnam, the Philippines claim extends past the legal authorities established by the 1982 UNCLOS for an exclusive economic zone. Similar to Vietnam, the Philippines claims the extended area as part of its EEZ, not as a territorial sea. The Philippines also claims portions of the Spratly Islands and this serves as the primary source of dispute between the Philippines and China. Unlike China and Vietnam, the Philippines has not attempted to colonize the islands. The Philippines places no claim on the Paracel Islands. The Philippines desires the extended area to improve the national economy. Expanding the EEZ of the Philippines enables the control of a larger portion of the plentiful fishing grounds west of the Philippines. The fishing industry provides a significant portion of the Philippines gross domestic product as well as nutritional needs for the country. Filipino fishermen continue to fish these grounds during the dispute leading to China firing on or confiscating many of the boats. China claims the Filipino

---

[30] Dong Manh Nguyen "Settlement of Disputes under the 1982 United Nations Convention On the Law of the Sea: The Case of the South China Sea Dispute," (December 2005): 14.

fishermen illegally fish the waters and violate Chinese law. These confrontations have not

resulted in a military on military confrontation between China and the Philippines to date. A

potential military confrontation between the Philippines and China could enable the Philippines to

invoke its mutual defense treaty with the United States of America. This mutual defense treaty is

one reason for involvement in the South China Sea dispute by the United States. In the absence of

asserting Chinese and Filipino claims through military force, each nation attempted to strengthen

its claim through other methods. China attempted to solidify its claim to ownership by stating that

the name of the region is the South China Sea and including the disputed region as part of China

on its new passports.[31] The Philippines renamed the area it claims as the West Philippines Sea to

counter the Chinese assertion, a name used by that United States Secretary of State Hillary

Clinton during a televised speech aboard an American warship anchored in Manila Bay.[32] Both

the Filipino and Chinese governments did not miss the symbolism of this speech and its location

leading to increased political posturing by both sides. Recently the Philippines indicated they

would take China to a UN tribunal to mediate the dispute. This represents a significant departure

from the mutually agreed solution desired in the 2002 ASEAN Declaration. The actions of

Vietnam, China, and the Philippines receive the majority of attention but one other nation extends

a claim over a portion of the islands in the South China Sea, Malaysia.[33]

Malaysia is the last country to claim any sovereignty over the Spratly Islands. Unlike the

three previous nations, Malaysia's claim only extends to the legal border of the EEZ under the

1982 UNCLOS. Based on this principle, Malaysia believes the islands that lie inside this

---

[31] "Philippines Will Not Stamp New China Passport," *Al-Jazeera Online,* November 29, 2012. http://www.aljazeera.com/news/asia-pacific/2012/11/2012112961659865875.html. (accessed January 29, 2013).

[32] Floyd Whaley, "Clinton Reaffirms Military Ties With the Philippines," *The New York Times Online.* November 17, 2011. http:// www.nytimes.com/2011/11/17/world/asia/clinton-reaffirms-military-ties-with-the-philippines.html?_r=0 (accessed January 29, 2013).

[33] U.S. Pacific Command, *South China Sea Reference Book* (Honolulu, HI, 1996), 10.

boundary are sovereign territory of Malaysia. The 1982 UNCLOS does not provide a method for a nation to claim sovereignty over landmasses inside their EEZ. The treaty only covers the legality of claims from inhabited areas and does not provide a provision for claiming uninhabited areas. Due to the extensive claims of China and Vietnam, both nations dispute Malaysia's claims (Malaysia and Philippines do not claim the same islands). As with the Philippines and Vietnam, Malaysia claims the area for economic reasons and does not extend its sovereignty past the twelve nautical miles as dictated by the 1982 UNCLOS. After Malaysia, two other ASEAN members claim portions of the South China Sea under the UNCLOS.[34]

Both Brunei and Indonesia claim portions of the South China Sea for their EEZ in accordance with the 1982 UNCLOS. Neither nation makes a formal or informal claim to the Spratly or Paracel Islands. They place claims for strictly for economic benefit and do not attempt to establish sovereignty. Due to the geographic proximity of the members of ASEAN, the EEZ of Brunei overlaps the EEZs of Indonesia, Malaysia, and the Philippines. The EEZ of Indonesia overlaps the EEZ of Malaysia, Brunei, Vietnam and the Philippine EEZ. Prior to adjudicating the conflicting claims with China, ASEAN could develop a consensus solution to resolve the overlapping claims of its member nations (Vietnam, the Philippines, Malaysia, Brunei, and Indonesia) based on the provisions in the 1982 UNCLOS. This would demonstrate to the world and China, ASEAN's desire to reach a consensus solution and could minimize the influence and involvement of the secondary actors. However, the lack of a common position when negotiating with China over the South China Sea decreases the legitimacy of ASEAN and enables the involvement of actors outside the region to help reach a solution. [35]

Of the primary actors identified, the dispute primarily revolves around the competing claims of China, Vietnam, and the Philippines. ASEAN's inability to solve the overlapping

---

[34] U.S. Pacific Command, *South China Sea Reference Book*, 9.

[35] Ibid., 10-11.

claims between its member states, the importance of the strategic lines of communication running through the South China Sea, and the potential economic benefit from oil and gas provide justification for involvement by the secondary actors. The inclusion of the secondary actors adds a layer of complexity to reaching a solution. This increased complexity makes it highly unlikely the nations will find a solution in the near or distant future.

Secondary Actors (Don't Border the SCS)

The inability of ASEAN to reach a solution among its member states concerning the overlapping claims decreases the legitimacy of ASEAN as an organizing body. Since the first ASEAN Summit in 1976, ASEAN members have always concluded their meeting by publishing a unanimous position on the matter presented to the ASEAN summit... This practice continued until the 20th ASEAN summit in 2012, when the body failed to adjudicate the overlapping claims in the South China Sea. ASEAN prided itself on its perfect record of agreement. The failure of ASEAN to unify its members in this instance led outside actors to become involved. As the primary actors look to increase the benefit gained from their individual claims, the remaining members of ASEAN along with the United States and India entered the dispute to formulate a solution in their respective interests. The interests of these nations add even more complexity to this dispute and significantly reduce the ability of ASEAN or another body to broker a solution. The actors in the secondary group primarily align themselves with Vietnam, China, or the Philippines. The secondary actors attempt to shape the solution to benefit their individual interests through support of one of the primary actors.

The strategic pivot to the Asia-Pacific region outlined in the 2012 National Defense Strategic Guidance focuses more attention from the United States on the South China Sea dispute than previously. While the United States does not directly border this area, it has significant interest in the movement of goods and personnel through the region. The United States wants the major sea line of communication running through the South China to remain international waters

23

and opposes national efforts to assert jurisdiction over the flow of these goods and personnel. The United States' continued involvement in the Middle East relies on the flow of equipment through this international waterway to support operations. In addition to diplomatic, economic, and military operations in the Middle East, the United States also possesses significant ties with countries bordering the South China Sea and with countries that receive a predominance of their supplies from the vessels that transit it. The United States has mutual defense treaties with the Philippines, Japan, and the Republic of Korea. Any attempt to disrupt the flow of resources through this area would negatively affect one or all of these allies. A threat to the flow of resources to Japan, the Philippines, or the Republic of Korea could lead to the invocation of a mutual defense treaty. These factors led the United States to support the Philippines and its claim. By supporting the Philippines claim against China, the United States looks to increase its influence in the region while simultaneously reducing China's influence. As the United States seeks to increase its influence inside the region through its support of the Philippines, India hopes to achieve the same condition by supporting Vietnam.[36]

One of the newest nations to enter the dispute is India. Like the rest of the secondary actors, it does not border the South China Sea. Similar to the other actors, India seeks to increase its economic and political influence in the region. To increase Indian economic influence, India has undertaken joint resource development projects with Vietnam in the South China Sea. These projects provide an economic boost to both countries and provide a cheaper supply of the petroleum resources required for developing a stronger industrial base inside each country. The involvement of Indian corporations in resource development in the South China Sea irks China. China presented similar joint development options to the members of ASEAN to enable joint resource development projects until China and the primary actors reached a permanent solution.

---

[36] Floyd Whaley, "Clinton Reaffirms Military Ties With the Philippines," *The New York Times Online.* November 17, 2011. http:// www.nytimes.com/2011/11/17/world/asia/clinton-reaffirms-military-ties-with-the-philippines.html?_r=0 (accessed January 29, 2013).

China responded to India's involvement in the South China Sea though harassment and interdiction of several Indian civilian or scientific research vessels. India's partnership with Vietnam ensures that any potential solution to the South China Sea must involve India. Collaborating with Vietnam allows India to improve its economy while simultaneously increasing its sphere of influence to the South China Sea. Improving the economy and extending political influence increase India's national power. These two objectives increase India's stature in Asia and challenges China's regional hegemony. The inclusion of India and its interests adds another layer of complexity to the South China Sea dispute.[37]

As Vietnam and the Philippines rely on the support of outside actors to improve their negotiating power, China relies on Cambodia to push the Chinese agenda. Cambodia recently supported Chinese desires to prevent internationalization of the South China Sea dispute. Cambodia also rebuked ASEAN members who involved nations from outside the region in the dispute. This rhetoric was a thinly veiled admonishment of the Philippines and Vietnam for their relationships with the United States and India respectively. China's partnership with Cambodia seeks to minimize the influence of India and the United States on a solution by branding those countries as outsiders and superfluous to a solution. Without the inclusion of the United States and India, China's economy, one measure of national power, is almost three and half times the size of the members of ASEAN collectively. Including the economies of the US and India with ASEAN creates an economic power in excess of two and half times the size of China.[38] Expanding these numbers to military expenditures shows how the involvement of the US and India reduce the power disparity between China and ASEAN. The Stockholm International Peace

---

[37] Jane Perlez, "Dispute Flares over Energy in South China Sea," *The New York Times Online.* December 4, 2012. http://www.nytimes.com/2012/12/05/world/asia/china-vietnam-and-india-fight-over-energy-exploration-in-south-china-sea.html (accessed January 3, 2013).

[38] The World Bank, "World Development Indicators," http://data.worldbank.org/data-catalog/GDP-ranking-table (accessed April 8, 2013).

Research Institute lists the US, China, and India as the world's first, second, and eighth largest spenders on defense. The removal of the US and India from this equation produces the same results as the economic comparison.[39] Removing the influence of the US and India increases the power disparity between China and the primary actors for China.[40]

The expected economic benefit each involved nation would receive underlies all parties' claims. However, while this dispute continues, no party can maximize the expected economic return. China claims the entirety of the region as part of their territorial sea limiting the ability of all nations to negotiate. The Chinese claim also allows them to dispute any attempted solution by ASEAN or other parties. The members of ASEAN have not solved their competing claims. Aside from China's desire for joint development of the region and the 2002 ASEAN Declaration, there is no evidence of additional attempts to resolve the competing claims. With the vast economic resources available in the South China Sea, the lack of a common solution or energy towards the creation of one requires explanation. Mancur Olson and Alan Lamborn both provided theories that help explain why the actors in the dispute disregard a common solution in favor of their individual claims.

REASONS FOR NO SOLUTION

Mancur Olson and Alan Lamborn have published concepts that help to explain why the nations involved cannot adopt a common policy on the South China Sea. *The Logic of Collective Action* presents Mancur Olson's findings from his study of motivations and interactions of actors inside a group working to achieve a collective economic purpose. Each group studied was an

---

[39] "Background paper on SIPRI military expenditure date, 2011," *Stockholm International Peace Research Institute Online*, April 17, 2012. http://www.sipri.org/research/armaments/milex/sipri-factsheet-on-military-expenditure-2011.pdf (accessed April 8, 2013).

[40] Jane Perlez, "China Stalls Move to Quell Asia Disputes Over Territory," *The New York Times Online.* November 19, 2012. http://www.nytimes.com/2012/11/20/world/asia/china-and-cambodia-stall-move-to-quell-disputes-in-southeast-asia.html (accessed January 3, 2013).

organization responsible for providing a common resource or service that increased each person's

individual benefits. Olson's findings directly apply to the South China Sea dispute. The primary

actors form a group responsible for reaching a collective solution for a common problem. The

natural and petroleum resources correspond to the collective resources and the economic benefit

considered by Olson. Olson's research questioned the common belief that groups comprised of

members with common interests make decisions that place the good of the whole over the good

of the individual member. According to Olson's research, the only way a group of individuals

reached a common, beneficial solution was through coercion. By coercion, Olson meant an

outside agent with the power to force the group to reach a solution. He clearly stated that a group

"will not act to advance their common or group objectives unless there is a threat of coercion."

Since no agent has attempted to coerce a solution for the South China Sea dispute, the dispute

continues as Olson's research indicated.[41] The principles asserted by Olson helped explain the

interactions of nations regarding economic interests. Because the primary actors are also nation-

states, Alan Lamborn's five political dynamics also help to explain the interaction of nation-

states.

Alan Lamborn developed five key dynamics he believed transcended the traditional

international relations theories of realism, neo-liberal institutionalism, and multilateralism. He

used the term dynamics to indicate that these fundamental political principles are the forces that

shape the political relationship between two nations. These dynamics exist at the level of meta-

theory and unify the different international relations theories. As the South China Sea dispute

comprises the interactions of individual nations with each other, Lamborn's five dynamics helped

provide an explanation of their interactions. The five critical dynamics were the interdependency

of power and preferences, the significance of legitimacy, variations in time horizons, variations in

---

[41] Mancur Olson, *The Logic of Collective Action: Public Goods and the Theory of Groups, Second Printing with New Preface and Appendix* (Harvard Economic Studies), Revised ed. (Cambridge, Mass.: Harvard University Press, 1971), 2.

risk taking preferences, and the impact of linkages. After determining the strategic importance of the South China Sea, analyzing the relevant documents regulating claims and their adjudication, and the various claims of the participants, using the works of Olson and Lamborn illustrated why ASEAN has failed to adopt a common policy on the South China Sea.

The Logic of Collective Action

An economist by trade, Mancur Olson studied theories about collective action and found the underlying premises false. In large groups, he found no mentality to sacrifice individual benefit for the good of the group. His studies showed that when a group has the potential to benefit equally from the development of a common resource, each individual member of the group will postpone a solution until they receive the majority if not all the benefits. The members of ASEAN exhibit this behavior in the South China Sea dispute. Economic growth was one of the founding principles of ASEAN and Olson's research explains the lack of a common solution from ASEAN.[42]

The potential economic gain from the exploration and development of hydrocarbon resources and increased fishing grounds comprise the economic benefits of the South China Sea. Before *The Logic of Collective Action*, common economic group theory predicted that the nations involved would reach a mutually beneficial solution. Each nation would receive an increase in economic benefits and quickly reach a solution. The duration of the South China Sea dispute supports the theory on collective action presented by Olson. Each side has determined to stall a solution until they receive maximum benefit. However, there is no ability to reach consensus if one nation or all the nations actively stall to increase their benefit.[43]

---

[42] Olson, *The Logic of Collective Action,* 16.

[43] Olson, *The Logic of Collective Action*, 35

The majority of observers wrongly view China as the main obstacle to reaching a solution concerning the South China Sea dispute. If true, all the other nations involved in the conflict would have resolved their competing claims, leaving their competing claim with China as the remaining obstacle. That is not the case. The expansive claim of China places them in a position of having competing claims with all the other nations surrounding the South China Sea. Yet China is not the sole nation with this claim. Vietnam's claim encompasses the same territorial breadth as China's, placing Vietnam in conflict with the same nations as China. Additionally, Malaysia, Indonesia, Brunei, and the Philippines all possess claims that overlap outside of the claims placed by China and Vietnam. The overlapping claims of the ASEAN members do not receive much publicity that reinforces the belief that the Chinese claim is the sole issue. Since the ASEAN members cannot reach a collective agreement among themselves, it is incorrect to conclude that the influence of China is the sole reason for the long unresolved dispute. The actions of the members of ASEAN correspond to the findings of Olson. As with the total South China Sea dispute, the members of ASEAN cannot reach a mutually agreed solution internally. Therefore, ASEAN cannot negotiate with China as one entity, which thereby decreases ASEAN's influence. The desire of all parties to obtain the best individual benefit is the primary impediment to a solution.[44]

The potential economic gain for each country involved in the South China Sea dispute provides the incentive required to extend the dispute. Each nation understands the positive impact their claim could have. This desire to achieve the greatest individual benefit is why there is no common solution between any of the parties involved. Olson's work provides a theoretical basis with which to explain the duration of the dispute. Each side will wait until they receive best-case scenario or until another actor creates a situation that forces a solution.

---

[44] Olson, *The Logic of Collective Action*, 43.

Five Political Dynamics

Lamborn presented five political dynamics that he believed explained the process of strategic interaction in politics."[45] The first political dynamic listed by Lamborn was the role of power and preferences. He defined power as relative between two nations and that this comparison was the only useful expression of power. Identification of the actor that possessed the relative power advantage only mattered when two actors in competition had different preferences for an outcome. He argued that if the actors have the same preferences for an outcome, then the importance of relative power diminishes since both actors desire a similar outcome. The work of Olson indicates that relative power is always important since actors desire to increase their individual positions at expense of a common solution. In the South China Sea dispute, all of the primary and secondary actors possess a different preference for a solution. Each nation wants to maximize their individual benefit at the expense of the group. According to Lamborn, because the preferences differ relative power becomes very important. Among the primary actors involved, China possesses the relative power advantage. China possesses greater economic and military power than each individual member of ASEAN and that of ASEAN as a whole. While China could easily defeat each of the primary actors to assert their claim to the South China Sea, the interest of the United States and India in this dispute dissuades China from this approach. Here the relative power of actors in the secondary group decreases the relative power of China. Additionally, the presence of the United States and India diminish the capabilities of China to exercise its relative power advantage over the other nations claiming portions of the South China Sea. This reinforces the weaker nations will to continue to attempt to maximize their individual benefit because while China possesses a relative power advantage it will not use it. Lamborn stressed this point in his article when he wrote "capabilities and power are not synonymous." The

---

[45] Alan C. Lamborn, "Theory and the Politics in World Politics," *International Studies Quarterly* 41, no. 2 (1997): 190. http://www.jstor.org/stable/3013931 (accessed October 19, 2012).

perceived legitimacy of the relationships between Vietnam and the Philippines with India and the United States respectively prevents China from translating its capabilities into power.[46]

The perceived legitimacy of the claims of other nations, the 1982 UNCLOS, the 2002 ASEAN Declaration, and the relationships between actors affects any potential solution for the South China Sea dispute. Each nation views its claim as legitimate and the competing or overlapping claims as illegitimate. This stance reinforces the findings of Olson and emphasizes the role of relative power by Lamborn. While attempting this solution, all parties cite the 1982 UNCLOS to legitimize their claims yet ASEAN does not leverage this to construct a solution. All of the primary actors in the dispute have ratified UNCLOS, meaning each party formally accepts the terms of the treaty. However, each nation refers only to the portions of the treaty that support their case while ignoring discrepancies between their claims and the terms of the treaty. As with the 1982 UNCLOS, each nation uses the 2002 ASEAN Declaration only when it supports their claim. Each head of state among the primary actors signed the declaration demonstrating their desire for a solution. Each nation uses the document to support its actions and argues against the actions and positions taken by other nations that contravene the terms of the declaration. Again, the governments ignore the portions of the declaration that they violate. China, the Philippines, and Vietnam recently attempted to place permanent settlements on the Spratly or Paracel Islands in direct violation of a portion of the 2002 ASEAN Declaration.[47] Additionally, the government of the Philippines announced it would request a UN Tribunal to adjudicate its dispute with China. This action also violated a tenet of the 2002 ASEAN Declaration that stated the involved parties would reach a solution internally.[48] The disparity between preferences for an outcome in the

---

[46] Lamborn, "Theory and the Politics in World Politics," 191.

[47] Ray Kwong, "Has the South China Sea Reached Boiling Point?," *Forbes Online,* July 24, 2012. http:// www.forbes.com/sites/raykwong/2012/07/24/has-the-south-china-sea-reached-boiling-point/ (accessed October 13, 2012).

[48] "Philippines 'to Take South China Sea Row to Court'" *BBC News*, January 22, 2013. http://www.bbc.co.uk/news/world-asia-21137144 (accessed January 29, 2013).

dispute and the perceived legitimacy of the guiding documents and actions of the involved

nations extend the time horizon for a permanent solution. Some actors in the dispute can afford to

wait for a more favorable solution while others cannot.

The concept of time horizons is Lamborn's third dynamic. Similar to the role of power

and preferences, the time horizons of the actors are shaped by policy preferences and each

government's perception of political risk. Lamborn defines policy risk as "the probability that

actors' substantive goals are not achieved" and defines political risk as "the probability that

policy choices will have adverse effects on the political position of the policy-making faction."[49]

In simpler terms, policy risk is the risk that a decision made by a decision maker fails to achieve

the desired end state. Political risk is a poor policy choice that removes the decision maker from

his position of influence. In the case of the South China Sea, China selects their political

leadership for a ten-year term. The leadership has very low political risk and, therefore, they can

assume higher policy risks. The armed conflicts with Filipino fisherman and Indian research

vessels demonstrate this. This also shows that China has the political power to wait for favorable

conditions for a Chinese solution. No country can remove the influence of China when framing a

solution. The lack of political risk creates China's long time horizon. In contrast to the Chinese

approach, the Filipino government has a different time horizon. The Filipino decision to request

for adjudication of its dispute with China through a UN Tribunal indicates a desire for a quicker

solution. In this case, the Filipino government has a shorter time horizon and faces increased

political risk the longer a resolution is delayed. The Philippine government reasons it is better to

achieve some of it demands through a UN tribunal than accept the political risk of popular

disaffection through further delay. In this example, the behavior of China and the Philippines

corresponds to the relationship presented by Lamborn concerning time horizons and their

---

[49] Alan C. Lamborn, "Theory and the Politics in World Politics," *International Studies Quarterly* 41, no. 2 (1997): 194. http://www.jstor.org/stable/3013931 (accessed October 19, 2012).

relationship to policy and political risk. The short time horizon and assumption of greater political risk faced by the Philippines compared to the long time horizon and minimal political risk faced by China illustrates the relationship between time horizons and risk taking preferences.

The longer a nation can wait for a solution in the South China Sea dispute, the less political risk its leadership takes. The opposite also applies. The quicker a nation wishes to reach a solution the greater political risk it must assume. In the South China Sea dispute, the risk spectrum is set for each country. Since no provision exists in the 1982 UNCLOS to force a solution, all parties involved could extend the dispute indefinitely. Olson's research indicates that these nations would only reach a solution to achieve maximum benefit or through coercion. The perpetuation of this conflict represents the lowest political risk for each country. As long as no country actively seeks a permanent solution then the rhetoric can continue. The Philippines recent actions support this. Threatening to take China to a UN Tribunal and actually taking China to the tribunal embody two separate risks. Conversely, forcing a solution represents the greatest political risk an actor can take. Any attempt to coerce a solution that fails instantly discredits the actor. In the South China Sea dispute, only one nation has the relative power to coerce the parties involved into a solution, the United States. However due to the substantial political risk involved, most notably the escalation of the dispute in an armed conflict with China, the United States will not assume this role. The desire of the United States to prevent the South China Sea dispute from escalating into a war is evidenced by the fact that the United States has failed to take a definitive position on what Chinese actions in the South China Sea mean concerning the mutual defense treaty the United States has with the Philippines.[50] Using the Lamborn's concepts to assess the risk to all nations presents the minimum political risk to all actors. None of the nations involved view the South China Sea dispute as an existential conflict in which they face eradication. They

---

[50] Steve Herman, "Philippines Looks to US Treaty in China Dispute," *Voice of America,* (May 23, 2012). http://www.voanews.com/articleprintview/925500.html (accessed January 13, 2013).

view it as a conflict over resources and regional power with little chance of escalation into a full-scale war. The relationships and linkages of the individual nations with one another truly mitigate the overall political risk in the South China Sea dispute.

The linkages between the members of ASEAN, China and Cambodia, Vietnam and India, and the Philippines and the United States create complexity that prevents a solution while also reducing the overall risk of the dispute. The link between China and Cambodia provides China the opportunity to influence ASEAN policy. The Philippines possess strong links to the United States decreasing the relative power of China over the Philippines. The Philippines and the United States also have a mutual defense treaty further reducing the Chinese advantage. Vietnam strengthened ties with India further balancing Chinese power. With the linkages in place, the South China Sea dispute has reached an equilibrium that all sides will attempt to maintain until reaching the conditions required for strengthening their claim.

CONCLUSION

The South China Sea possesses significant strategic value. The sea's estimated hydrocarbon resources, fishing stocks and shipping trade flows make it one of the most geographically important areas in the Pacific. The economic benefit from controlling this area led the nations surrounding the South China Sea to extend a variety of claims to the sea and its shoals, reefs, and islands. Due to the geography of the South China Sea, these claims overlap and have created the framework for the South China Sea dispute.

Between 1973 and 1982, the Third United Nations Convention on the Law of the Sea attempted to delineate a boundary on national maritime claims. The final treaty produced in 1982 regulates current claims. China, Vietnam, the Philippines, Malaysia, Indonesia, and Brunei have all ratified the 1982 UNCLOS. However, both Chinese and Vietnamese claims currently exceed the legal limits established by the 1982 UNCLOS. The 1982 UNCLOS also provided three separate methods for resolving disputes. Yet none of the aforementioned nations has resolved their disputes in accordance with the 1982 UNCLOS. The lack of progress towards a permanent solution led to the signing of the 2002 ASEAN Declaration on the Conduct of Parties in the South China Sea. As with the 1982 UNCLOS, each of the primary actors signed this document. This political statement attempted to prevent escalation of the dispute and demonstrate the willingness of all parties to find a solution. The repeated attempts by China and Vietnam to establish settlements on the Spratly Islands and the recent statement by the Philippines declaring its desire to take China to a UN tribunal to adjudicate their mutual claims all stand counter to the terms of the ASEAN declaration. The theories of Mancur Olson and Alan Lamborn helped explain the economic and political motivations of each nation in this dispute and their reluctance to reach a common solution.

Olson studied how competing economic objectives affected the ability to reach a solution. At the time of his study, the prevailing theory stated that in groups where each individual member received benefits from a common resource, the group acted as a collective whole to reach a mutually beneficial solution. Olson challenged that assertion. He argued that parties would not seek a mutually beneficial collective solution but would rather seek a solution achieving the highest possible individual benefit. Analyzing the South China Sea dispute through Olson's theory, it became easy to see why the thirteen nations involved have failed to produce a solution. Most significant was ASEAN's inability to adjudicate a solution between its members. One of ASEAN's founding principles was economic growth for its members but ASEAN has been unable to reach a solution among its member that fosters growth. Alan Lamborn's five political dynamics also helped explain the political reasons for ASEAN's failure.

Alan Lamborn's five political dynamics explain the interactions of political actors. Applied to the South China Sea dispute, these dynamics helped interpret the actions of ASEAN's members. The role of power and preferences helped set the structure of the dispute. Since the nations have competing preferences, relative power plays a more dominant role. Among the primary actors, China possesses the greatest national power and under Olson's theory could

35

coerce the other actors into a solution. Here the role of linkages helps offset the relative power advantage of China. The involvement of the United States and India in this dispute diminishes the ability of China to exercise power over the members of ASEAN. The role of linkages coupled with the fact that the nations involved do not view the other claims as legitimate prolongs this dispute. In the case of China and Vietnam, not only do they feel their individual claims are the sole legitimate claims, they view their claims as superior to any claims made under the 1982 UNCLOS. The harassment of Filipino fishing vessels and civilian research vessels demonstrates China's willingness to accept greater policy risk. Since each nation awaits a solution that provides maximum individual benefit, this situation has no near term solution.

It is unlikely there will be any quick resolution to the claims in the South China Sea. The potential value of the claim drives the competing states to pursue a national rather than a collective settlement. Under current circumstances, a collective settlement could only emerge under the auspices of an outside third party. Since the United States and India show no inclination to assume the role of honest broker, the situation in the South China Sea will fester for years to come.

BIBLIOGRAPHY

Argentina, Austria, Belgium, Bolivia, Brazil, etc. September 8, 1951. "Treaty of Peace with Japan (with two declarations)." San Francisco, Chapter 2, Article 2(f) (1951).

Association of Southeast Asian Nations. "History." http://www.asean.org/asean/about-asean/history, (accessed October 10, 2012).

"Background paper on SIPRI military expenditure date, 2011," *Stockholm International Peace Research Institute Online*, April 17, 2012. http://www.sipri.org/research/armaments/milex/sipri-factsheet-on-military-expenditure-2011.pdf (accessed April 8, 2013).

Bensurto Jr., Henry S. "Cooperative Architecture in the South China Sea: Asean-China Zone of Peace, Freedom, Friendship, and Cooperation." http://csis.org/files/publication/110630_Bensurto.pdf (accessed December 13, 2012).

Brzezinski, Zbignew. "Balancing the East, Upgrading the West." *Foreign Affairs* (January/February 2012): 97-104.

Buszynski, Leszek. "The South China Sea: Oil, Maritime Claims, and U.S. – China Strategic Rivalry." *The Washington Quarterly*, vol. 35, no. 2 (2012): 139-156. http://csis.org/files/publication/twq12springbuszynski.pdf (accessed August 21, 2012).

Clinton, Hillary. "America's Pacific Century." *Foreign Policy* (November 2011): 56-63.

Chiang, Frank. "Abusing History?" *The Diplomat*. October 16, 2011. http://thediplomat.com/2011/10/16/abusing-history/ (accessed August 14, 2012).

Coonen, Steve. "The Empire's Newest New Clothes: Overrating China." *Joint Forces Quarterly*, Issue 63, 4th Edition (2011): 84-91.

Craig, Susan L. "Chinese Perceptions of Traditional and Nontraditional Security Threats." Carlisle Barracks Strategic Plans Institute, March 2007.

Cronin, Patrick M., ed. "Cooperation from Strength: The United States, China and the South China Sea." *Center for a New American Security*. January 2012. http://www.cnas.org/southchinasea (accessed August 19, 2012).

Davis, Elizabeth Van Wie. "Governance in China in 2010." *Asian Affairs: An American Review* (2009), 195-211.

Department of Defense. "Annual Report to Congress on Military and Security Development Involving the People's Republic of China." Washington, D.C. May 2012.

Hau, Yufan, C.X. George Wei, and Lowell Dittmer, Ed. *Challenges to Chinese Foreign Policy: Diplomacy, Globalization, and the Next World Power.* Lexington: University of Kentucky Press, 2009.

Herman, Steve. "Philippines Looks to US Treaty in China Dispute." *Voice of America*. May 23, 2012. http://www.voanews.com/articleprintview/925500.html (accessed January 13, 2013).

Ikenberry, G. John. "The Rise of China and the Future of the West." *Foreign Affairs*, May/June 2010.

Jijun, Lieutenant General Li. "Traditional Military Thinking and the Defensive Strategy of China." Carlisle Barracks: Strategic Studies Institute, August 1997.

Kaplan, Robert D. "The South China Sea is the Future of Conflict." *Foreign Policy*. Sep/Oct 2011. http://www.foreignpolicy.com/articles/2011/08/15/the_south_china_sea_is_the_future_of_conflict

Keck, Zachary. "China and America's Dueling South China Sea Statements." *The Diplomat*. August 7, 2012. http://thediplomat.com/china-power/china-and-americas-dueling-south-china-sea-statements/ (accessed August 14, 2012)

Kissinger, Henry. *On China*. New York: Penguin Press, 2011.

Kwong, Ray. "Has The South China Sea Reached Boiling Point?" *Forbes Online*. July 24, 2012. http: www.forbes.com/sites/raykwong/2012/07/24/has-the-south-china-sea-reached-boiling-point/ (accessed October 13, 2012).

Lai, David. "Learning from the Stones: a GO Approach to Mastering China's Strategic Concept, Shi." Carlisle Barracks: Strategic Studies Institute, May 2004.

Lamborn, Alan C. "Theory and the Politics in World Politics." *International Studies Quarterly 41*, no. 2 (1997): 187-214. http://www.jstor.org/stable/3013931 (accessed October 19, 2012).

Liang, Colonel Qiao and Colonel Wang Xiangsui. *Unrestricted Warfare: China's Mater Plan to Destroy America*. Panama City, Panama: Pan American Publishing Company, 2002.

Liu, Guoli, Ed. *Chinese Foreign Policy in Transition*. New York: Aldine de Gruyter, 2004.

Olson, Mancur. *The Logic of Collective Action: Public Goods and the Theory of Groups, Second Printing with New Preface and Appendix* (Harvard Economic Studies). Revised ed. Cambridge, Mass.: Harvard University Press, 1971.

Perlez, Jane. "China Stalls Move to Quell Asia Disputes Over Territory." *The New York Times Online*. December 4, 2012. http:// http://www.nytimes.com/2012/11/20/world/asia/china-and-cambodia-stall-move-to-quell-disputes-in-southeast-asia.html (accessed January 3, 2013).

Perlez, Jane. "Dispute Flares over Energy in South China Sea." *The New York Times Online*. December 4, 2012. http://www.nytimes.com/2012/05/world/asia/china-vietnam-and-india-fight-over-exploration-in-south-china-sea.html (accessed January 3, 2013).

"Philippines 'to Take South China Sea Row to Court'" *BBC News*, January 22, 2013. http://www.bbc.co.uk/news/world-asia-21137144 (accessed January 29, 2013).

"Philippines Will Not Stamp New China Passport." *Al-Jazeera Online*. November 29, 2012. http://www.aljazeera.com/news/asia-pacific/2012/11/2012112961659865875.html (accessed January 29, 2013).

Scobell, Andrew. *China and Strategic Culture*. Carlisle Barracks: Strategic Studies Institute, May 2002.

Shen, Jianming. "China's Sovereignty over the South China Sea Islands: A Historical Perspective." *Chinese Journal of International Law* (2002): 94-157. http://chinesejil.oxfordjournals.org/content/1/1/94.full.pdf (accessed August 21, 2012).

Sutter, Robert G. *China's Rise in Asia*. Lanham, Maryland: Rowman and Littlefield Publishers, INC., 2005.

Thang, Nguyen-Dang and Nguyen Hong Thao. "China's nine dotted lines in the South China Sea: the 2011 exchange of diplomatic notes between the Philippines and China." *Ocean Development and International Law*, vol. 43, no. 1 (Jan-Mar 2012): 35-57.

Whaley, Floyd. "Clinton Reaffirms Military Ties With the Philippines." *The New York Times Online*. November 17, 2011. http://www.nytimes.com/2011/11/17/world/asia/clinton-reaffirms-military-ties-with-the-philippines.html?_r=0 (accessed January 29, 2013).

The World Bank, "World Development Indicators," http://data.worldbank.org/data-catalog/GDP-ranking-table (accessed April 8, 2013).